C0-AWP-351

Illustration by Maryann Fennimore

America's
HOME COOKING

COOKIES

WQED
Multimedia

A production of WQED Multimedia

For other great merchandise visit Shop WQED at www.wqed.org, or call
1-800-274-1307, or write to Shop WQED, 4802 Fifth Avenue, Pittsburgh, PA 15213

Table of Contents

Table of Contents

Table of Contents

Drop Cookies

Anise Butter Cookies

DIRECTIONS

Preheat oven to 375 degrees. Cream butter. Gradually add sugar, anise seed, vanilla and salt. Blend in flour. Shape into balls, roll into granulated sugar and place on a greased cookie sheet. Flatten with a glass dipped in sugar. Decorate with red or green cherries, if desired. Bake at 375 degrees for 12 to 14 minutes. Yield 5 dozen.

INGREDIENTS

1 cup butter

1/2 cup sugar

1/2 teaspoon crushed anise seed

1 teaspoon vanilla

1/4 teaspoon salt

2 cups flour

granulated sugar for rolling

red and green cherries for decorating, optional

SUBMITTED BY:

Mrs. Frances Sbarro, Wampum

Apple Butter Cookies

DIRECTIONS

Preheat oven to 375 degrees; grease cookie sheets. Sift flour, baking powder, baking soda and salt into a mixer bowl. Add butter, and stir until well blended. Beat in brown sugar, egg, apple butter and milk. Mix well. Add oats and raisins; mix well. Drop by teaspoonful onto prepared cookie sheets. Bake 15 minutes or until golden. Yield: 3 dozen

INGREDIENTS

1 cup flour

1/2 teaspoon baking powder

1/2 teaspoon baking soda

1/2 teaspoon salt

1/4 cup (1/2 stick) butter, softened

2/3 cup brown sugar, packed

1 egg, beaten

1/2 cup apple butter

2 tablespoons milk

1 cup rolled oats

1 cup raisins

SUBMITTED BY:
Nancy Otto, Indiana

Applesauce Cookies

DIRECTIONS

Preheat oven to 375 degrees. Combine all
ingredients and drop by spoonful onto well-
greased cookie sheets. Bake for 5-10 minutes.
Yields 6 1/2 dozen. Cookies stay moist and
fruity.

INGREDIENTS

1 cup thick applesauce

1/2 cup margarine or butter

1 cup chopped raisins

1 cup chopped nuts

2 cups flour

1 teaspoon cloves

1 teaspoon cinnamon

1 cup sugar

1 egg

1/2 teaspoon salt

1 teaspoon soda

1 teaspoon baking powder

SUBMITTED BY:
Leah Dallasen, St. Mary

Apricot Jewels

DIRECTIONS

Sift together flour, sugar, baking powder and salt into mixing bowl. Cut in butter and cream cheese; add coconut and apricot preserves. Blend well and chill overnight.

Preheat oven to 350 degrees. Drop by teaspoon onto ungreased cookie sheets. Bake at 350 degrees 15-18 minutes until light brown. Cool and frost. Decorate with coconut, if desired.

Frosting: Combine all ingredients and beat until smooth. Makes 2 1/2 dozen.

INGREDIENTS

1 1/4 cup flour
1/4 cup sugar
1 1/2 teaspoons baking powder
1/4 teaspoon salt
1/2 cup butter
3 oz package cream cheese
1/2 cup coconut
1/2 cup apricot preserves

Apricot Frosting:
1 cup sifted powdered sugar
1 tablespoon soft butter
1/4 cup apricot preserves

SUBMITTED BY:
Rosemary Casselman, Allison Park

Armed Forces Cookies

DIRECTIONS

Preheat oven to 375 degrees. Mix shortening, sugar and egg until creamy. Sift together flour, baking soda, salt, cinnamon and nutmeg. Add to the creamy mixture. Add walnuts, chocolate chips, coconut, raisins and bananas. Stir in rolled oats. Drop dough off the end of a teaspoon onto a lightly greased cookie sheet. Bake at 375 degrees for 12 minutes. Makes about 75 cookies.

INGREDIENTS

3/4 cup shortening

1 cup brown sugar

1 egg

1 1/2 cup flour

1/2 teaspoon baking soda

1 teaspoon salt

1 teaspoon cinnamon

1/4 teaspoon nutmeg

1/2 cup walnuts

1/2 cup mint flavored chocolate chips

1/2 cup coconut

1/2 cup raisins
1 cup mashed ripe bananas (2 or 3 bananas)

1 3/4 cups rolled oats

SUBMITTED BY:
Margaret Evanichko, Latrobe

Banana Nut Cookies

DIRECTIONS

Preheat oven to 375 degrees. Combine flour, baking soda, baking powder and salt. In a separate bowl, cream together butter and sugar. Beat in eggs and banana extract. Gradually add pudding mix. Gradually add flour mixture; stir in chopped walnuts. Drop by heaping teaspoonful on a baking sheet. Bake at 375 degrees for 9 1/2 to 10 minutes. Do not overbake.

INGREDIENTS

2 1/4 cups flour

1 teaspoon baking soda

1/4 teaspoon baking powder

1/2 teaspoon salt

1 cup (2 sticks) butter or margarine

3/4 cup light brown sugar

2 eggs

1 teaspoon banana extract

3.4 oz package banana instant pudding

1 or 1 1/2 cups chopped walnuts

SUBMITTED BY:
Lois Wolfe, Smithfield

11

Bushel Basket Cookies

DIRECTIONS

Preheat oven to 350 degrees; grease cookie sheets. Mix all ingredients well. Drop dough with teaspoon onto cookie sheets. Bake until browned.

INGREDIENTS

2 cups shortening

1 1/2 cups brown sugar

1 1/2 cups white sugar

2 teaspoons vanilla extract

3 eggs

3 1/2 cups flour

1 teaspoon salt

1 teaspoon baking powder

3 cups oatmeal

2 cups crushed corn flakes

2 cups chopped nuts

1 teaspoon baking soda

SUBMITTED BY:
Ethelclaire Smith, Smithton

Canadian Shortbread

DIRECTIONS

Mix butter, sugar and vanilla until fluffy. In a separate bowl, blend flour, soda and oatmeal. Stir into butter mixture. Shape dough into rolls and wrap in waxed paper; chill for 1 to 2 hours. Preheat oven to 350 degrees. Slice dough; bake slices for 10 to 12 minutes.

INGREDIENTS

1 cup (2 sticks) butter

1/2 cup brown sugar

1 teaspoon vanilla extract

1 cup flour

1/2 teaspoon baking soda

2 cups quick cooking oatmeal

SUBMITTED BY:
Margaret Meister, Pittsburgh

Carrot Cookies with Orange Icing

DIRECTIONS

Preheat oven to 400 degrees. Cream shortening and sugar in large bowl until light and fluffy. Beat in eggs, carrots and orange flavoring until well blended. Sift flour, baking powder and salt. Gradually add flour mixture to creamed ingredients; beat until well mixed. Stir in coconut. Drop dough by rounded teaspoon onto greased cookie sheet. Bake at 400 degrees for 8-10 minutes until very lightly browned and cookie springs back when touched lightly with a finger. Remove from cookie sheet to cool.

Orange Icing: Mix together icing ingredients until creamy; add orange juice and flavoring until smooth. Stir in coconut. Frost cooled cookies. Yields 5-6 dozen.

INGREDIENTS

1 cup butter-flavor shortening

3/4 cup sugar

2 eggs

2/3 cup cooked, mashed carrots

orange oil, extract or flavoring to taste

2 cups flour

2 teaspoons baking powder

1/2 teaspoon salt

3/4 to 1 cup coconut

Orange Icing:

1 1/2 cups powdered sugar

3 tablespoons softened margarine

2 tablespoons fresh orange juice

1 teaspoon grated fresh orange rind

orange oil, flavoring to taste

3/4 to 1 cup coconut

SUBMITTED BY:

Susan R. Tenney, Mather

Chocolate Chip Cookies with Sour Cream

DIRECTIONS

Preheat oven to 375 degrees; grease cookie sheets. Sift together flour, salt, baking powder and baking soda. In a separate bowl, cream margarine and sugar together. Add eggs and vanilla; mix well. Add sifted dry ingredients alternately with sour cream. Add chopped nuts and chocolate pieces; blend. Drop by teaspoon on a greased cookie sheet. Bake for 7-10 minutes or until brown. Remove from cookie sheet at once, cool on cake rack. Make a soft cookie, not hard.

INGREDIENTS

2 1/2 cups flour

1/2 teaspoon salt

1/2 teaspoon baking powder

1 teaspoon baking soda

1/2 cup margarine

1 1/2 cups light or dark brown sugar

2 eggs

1 teaspoon vanilla extract

1 cup sour cream

1 cup chopped nuts

12 oz package semi-sweet chocolate bits

SUBMITTED BY:
Reda Addis, Grindstone

15

America's
HOME COOKING

Chocolate Crinkles

DIRECTIONS

Combine sugar and oil. Add cocoa, blend well. Beat in eggs and vanilla. Combine flour, baking powder and salt; add to cocoa mixture, blending well. Cover and chill for 4 hours or overnight.

Preheat oven to 350 degrees. Shape dough into 2 inch balls. Roll each ball in powdered sugar. Place 3 inches apart on greased cookie sheet. Bake at 350 degrees 16-18 minutes. Remove from cookie sheet; cool on wire rack. Makes about 20 cookies.

INGREDIENTS

2 cups sugar

3/4 cup oil

3/4 cup cocoa

4 eggs

2 teaspoons vanilla

2 1/3 cups flour

2 teaspoons baking powder

1/2 teaspoon salt

Powdered sugar

SUBMITTED BY:
Margaret Evanichko, Latrobe

America's HOME COOKING

Chocolate Orange Crunchies

DIRECTIONS

Preheat oven to 350 degrees. Blend shortening, salt, rind and juice. Add sugar and egg; beat well. Sift flour with baking soda and salt. Add to creamed mixture; mix thoroughly. Add nuts and chocolate chips. Drop from tablespoon on greased cookie sheet. Bake at 350 degrees for 15 minutes.

INGREDIENTS

1 cup shortening

1 1/4 teaspoons salt

1 tablespoon orange rind

2 tablespoons orange juice

2/3 cup brown sugar

1 egg

2 cups flour

1/2 teaspoon baking soda

1/4 teaspoon salt

1/2 cup nuts

6 oz package chocolate chips

SUBMITTED BY:
Viewer from Pittsburgh

Chopped Apple Cookies

DIRECTIONS

Preheat oven to 400 degrees. Boil raisins for three minutes, drain and set aside. Cream together shortening and brown sugar until fluffy. Add egg; mix well. Sift flour, soda, salt, cinnamon, cloves and nutmeg; add to shortening mixture. Add milk; mix well. Add chopped apples, raisins and nuts last. Drop by teaspoon on ungreased cookie sheet. Bake at 400 degrees for 8-10 minutes. While still warm, glaze with a mix of powdered sugar and milk.

INGREDIENTS

1 cup raisins
1/2 cup shortening
1 1/3 cup brown sugar
1 egg, beaten
2 cups all-purpose flour
1 teaspoon soda
1/2 teaspoon salt
1 teaspoon cinnamon
1 teaspoon cloves
1/2 teaspoon nutmeg
1/4 cup milk
1 cup peeled, chopped apples
1 cup chopped nuts

Glaze:
Powdered sugar
Milk

SUBMITTED BY:
Beckie Wagner, Masontown

America's
HOME COOKING

Christmas Fruitcake Cookies

DIRECTIONS

Preheat oven to 400 degrees. Sift together flour, baking soda, salt and cinnamon. Cream butter; add eggs and sugar. Stir the flour combination, nuts and fruit into the butter mixture. Drop from teaspoon on cookie sheet; bake for 10 minutes. Do not overbake.

INGREDIENTS

2 1/2 cups sifted flour

1 teaspoon baking soda

1 teaspoon salt

1 teaspoon cinnamon

1 cup (2 sticks) butter or margarine

2 eggs

1 1/2 cups sugar

2 pounds dates, chopped

1/2 pound candied cherries, chopped

1/2 pound candied pineapple, chopped

1/2 pound shelled almonds, chopped

1/2 pound shelled hazelnuts, chopped

SUBMITTED BY:
Detty Geracia, Oakmont

Coconut Crunchies

DIRECTIONS

Preheat oven to 325 degrees. Combine first 3 ingredients in a large bowl and cream together. Add remaining ingredients and mix well. Drop by teaspoon on greased cookie sheet. Bake 13-15 minutes at 325 degrees. Cookies will not brown.

INGREDIENTS

1 cup margarine, softened

1 cup white sugar

1 cup brown sugar

1/2 teaspoon baking soda

1/4 teaspoon salt

2 cups corn flakes

1 teaspoon vanilla

2 eggs

2 cups flour

1 teaspoon baking powder

2 cups quick rolled oats

1 cup coconut

SUBMITTED BY:

Viewer from Pittsburgh

Corn Flake Macaroons

DIRECTIONS

Melt butter in quart saucepan. Stir in sugar and evaporated milk until well blended. Cook mixture over medium heat until it reached a full, all-over boil then boil for 2 minutes. Take from heat and stir in coconut, corn flakes, nuts and vanilla. With teaspoon, drop mixture onto a greased cooking pan. Let stand at room temperature until set. Makes about 2 dozen.

INGREDIENTS

1/4 cup butter or margarine

3/4 cup sugar

1/4 cup evaporated milk

1 cup canned flaked coconut

1 1/2 cups corn flakes

1/2 cup unsalted nuts, chopped

1/2 teaspoon vanilla

SUBMITTED BY:

Ann Isabella, New Castle

Frosty Apple Bites

DIRECTIONS

Preheat oven to 375 degrees. Sift together flour, soda, salt and nutmeg. In another bowl, cream butter; gradually add brown sugar. Blend in unbeaten egg and vanilla. Add flour mixture alternately with evaporated milk, beginning and ending with flour mixture and blending well after each addition. Stir in walnuts, apples and chocolate morsels. Drop by teaspoon onto greased cookie sheet. Bake at 375 degrees for 12-15 minutes. Frost while warm.

Cinnamon Glaze: Combine sifted powdered sugar with melted butter and cinnamon. Add evaporated milk until of spreading consistency.

INGREDIENTS

2 cups sifted all purpose flour
1/2 teaspoon soda
1/2 teaspoon salt
1/4 teaspoon nutmeg
1/4 cup butter
1 cup firmly packed brown sugar
1 unbeaten egg
1 teaspoon vanilla
2/3 cup evaporated milk
1 cup walnuts, chopped
1 cup pared, chopped apples
1/2 cup chocolate morsels

Cinnamon Glaze:
2 cups sifted powdered sugar
3 tablespoons melted butter
1 teaspoon cinnamon
2-3 tablespoons evaporated milk for consistency

SUBMITTED BY:
Annabelle Thomas, Pittsburgh

Giant Trail Mix Cookies

DIRECTIONS

Preheat oven to 375 degrees. In a medium bowl mix flour, cereal, baking soda and salt; set aside. In large bowl mix the sugars, coconut, oil, vanilla and eggs until blended. Stir in blended dry ingredients. With hands, roll 1/2 cup dough into balls, placing them on cookie sheets about 3 inches apart, flattening them slightly. Press several M&M's gently into the tops of cookies. Bake 10 to 12 minutes or until golden; cool on wire racks. Makes 18 large cookies.

INGREDIENTS

2 1/4 cups all-purpose flour

2 cups granola cereal with raisins

1 teaspoon baking soda

1 teaspoon salt

3/4 cup sugar

1/2 cup packed light brown sugar

3/4 cup flaked coconut

2/3 cup vegetable oil

2 teaspoons vanilla extract

2 large eggs

1/2 cup plain M&M's

SUBMITTED BY:
Barbara Houston, Pittsburgh

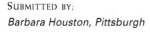

23

Ginger Creams

DIRECTIONS

Mix thoroughly shortening, sugar, egg, molasses and water. Blend in remaining ingredients. Cover, chill 1 hour.

Heat oven to 400 degrees. Drop dough by teaspoonfuls two inches apart onto ungreased cookies sheet. Bake 8 minutes or until almost no imprint remains when touched with finger. Immediately remove from baking sheet; cool.

Frosting: Blend butter and sugar. Stir in vanilla and milk; beat until frosting is smooth and of spreading consistency.

INGREDIENTS

1/3 cup shortening

1/2 cup sugar

1 egg

1/2 cup molasses

1/2 cup water

2 cups all purpose flour

1 teaspoon ginger

1/2 teaspoon salt

1/2 teaspoon baking soda

1/2 teaspoon nutmeg

1/2 teaspoon cloves

1/2 teaspoon cinnamon

Frosting:

1/3 cup soft butter or margarine

3 cups powdered sugar

1 1/2 teaspoons vanilla

About 2 tablespoons milk

SUBMITTED BY:
Connie Hutchinson, Boswell, PA

Gingersnap Cookies with Lemon Icing

DIRECTIONS

Mix together the butter and both sugars until light and fluffy. Add molasses and beat until smooth. Add egg and beat until smooth. In another bowl, whisk together the flour, ginger, cinnamon, allspice, baking soda and salt. Add the flour mixture to the butter mixture until the dough forms a soft, gooey ball. Chill for 30 minutes. Preheat oven to 350 degrees. Form dough into 24 balls and place 2 inches apart on cookie sheet. Or make balls smaller and get 36 cookies. Bake for 13-15 minutes in middle of oven.

Lemon Icing:

Combine all ingredients until smooth. Frost cooled cookies and garnish with chopped pistachio nuts if desired.

INGREDIENTS

1/2 cup (1 stick) softened butter

1/2 cup granulated sugar

1/2 cup brown sugar, firmly packed

1/3 cup molasses

1 large egg

2 cups all purpose flour

3 teaspoons ground ginger

1/2 teaspoon cinnamon

1/4 teaspoon ground allspice

1 teaspoon baking soda

3/4 teaspoon salt

Lemon Icing:

1 teaspoon lemon rind

1/3 cup soft butter

1/3 cup fresh lemon juice

few drops of yellow food coloring

4 cups powdered sugar, sifted
chopped pistaschio nuts, if desired

SUBMITTED BY:
Antoinette Jucha

America's
HOME COOKING

Gold Carrot Cookies

DIRECTIONS

Preheat oven to 400 degrees. Mix butter, eggs, sugar and carrots. Add flour, baking powder, and salt into butter mix. Mix in coconut. Drop dough by teaspoon 2 inches apart on lightly greased cookie sheet. Bake at 400 degrees for 8-10 minutes.

INGREDIENTS

1 cup butter or oleo

2 eggs

3/4 cup sugar

1 cup mashed, cooked carrots

2 cups flour

2 teaspoons baking powder

1/2 teaspoon salt

3/4 cup shredded coconut

SUBMITTED BY:

Charlotte Hogel, Pittsburgh

Molasses Krinkles

DIRECTIONS

Cream shortening. Blend in sugar, egg, and molasses. Sift together flour, baking soda, salt and spices. Add to the creamed mixture. Mix well and chill at least an hour.

Preheat oven to 350 degrees. Form dough into balls the size of walnuts. Dip in sugar. Place sugar side up on cookie sheet, sprinkling each cookie with a couple drops of water. Bake at 350 degrees 10-12 minutes

INGREDIENTS

3/4 cup shortening

1 cup brown sugar

1 egg, beaten

4 tablespoons molasses

2 1/4 cups flour

2 teaspoons baking soda

1/2 teaspoon salt

1/2 teaspoon cloves

1 teaspoon cinnamon

1 teaspoon ginger

sugar for dipping

SUBMITTED BY:
Viewer from Pittsburgh

America's
HOME COOKING

Orange Drop Cookies

DIRECTIONS

Preheat oven to 350 degrees. Cream brown sugar and butter; add eggs, orange peel and vanilla. Beat until fluffy. Sift together flour, baking powder, baking soda and salt. Add to creamed mixture alternately with the buttermilk, beating after each addition. Drop onto cookie sheet, and bake for 10 to 12 minutes. While cookies are warm, frost with orange icing. Makes about six dozen cookies.

Icing: Combine all ingredients, mix well.

INGREDIENTS

1/2 cup packed brown sugar

1 cup (2 sticks) butter or margarine

2 eggs

1 tablespoon grated orange peel

1 teaspoon vanilla extract

3 cups sifted all-purpose flour

2 teaspoons baking powder

1 teaspoon baking soda

1/2 teaspoon salt

3/4 cup buttermilk

Orange Icing

1 tablespoon grated orange peel

3 tablespoons orange juice

3 tablespoons butter

3 cups sifted powdered sugar

SUBMITTED BY:
Cecelia Collins, Everson

Pecan Shortbread

DIRECTIONS

Preheat oven to 350 degrees. Cream butter, gradually add sugar, beating until light and fluffy. Sift together flour and salt; add to creamed mixture. Add more flour, if needed, to make dough easy to handle. Shape dough into 3/4 inch balls, place 2 inches apart on greased cookie sheet. Gently press a pecan half in center of each. Bake at 350 degrees for 8-10 minutes or until lightly browned. Roll in powdered sugar while warm. Makes 6 dozen.

INGREDIENTS

2 cups butter

1 cup sugar

4 cups flour

1/2 teaspoon salt

Pecan halves

Sifted powdered sugar

SUBMITTED BY:

LuAnne Salak, New Castle

Pumpkin Cookies

DIRECTIONS

Preheat oven to 375 degrees. Cream sugar, shortening, pumpkin and vanilla in bowl. Sift together dry ingredients and add to creamed mixture. Add nuts and raisins. Drop by teaspoon onto a cookie sheet; bake in 375 degree oven to 15-20 minutes. Makes 4 dozen cookies.

INGREDIENTS

1 cup sugar

1/2 cup shortening

1 cup canned pumpkin

1 teaspoon vanilla

1/2 teaspoon cinnamon

2 cups flour

1 teaspoon baking powder

1 teaspoon baking soda

1/2 cup nuts, chopped

1/2 cup raisins

SUBMITTED BY:

Charlotte Hogel, Pittsburgh

Raggedy Ann Cookies

DIRECTIONS

Arrange oven rack on second rung; preheat oven to 350 degrees. Rinse raisins and drain them; dry on paper towel. Cream sugar and margarine together; add eggs. Mix well. Add raisins, flour, vanilla, cornflakes, baking soda and coconut. Stir to blend. Drop by small spoonfuls on a cookie sheet 2 inches apart. Slightly flatten with fork. Bake for 11 to 12 minutes, or until golden brown.

INGREDIENTS

1 cup light raisins

1 cup sugar

1/2 cup margarine

2 eggs, well beaten

1 1/2 cups sifted flour

1 teaspoon vanilla extract

4 cups cornflakes

1/2 teaspoon baking soda

1 cup shredded coconut

SUBMITTED BY:
Mrs. Julia Bonifati, North Huntingdon

31

Rick's Big Old Cookies

DIRECTIONS

Preheat oven to 350 degrees. Mash together the butter and margarine. Add sugars and eggs; mix well. Add flour, baking soda and baking powder. Mix in vanilla. Then add in oatmeal, cereal, chocolate chips, raisins, chopped dates and white chocolate chips.

The dough should be really thick and full of stuff. Make golf ball sized balls for bigger cookies, smaller for smaller cookies. Bake at 350 for 15-20 minutes or until they are just golden. Makes a lot.

INGREDIENTS

1 cup (2 sticks) butter, softened

1 cup (2 sticks) margarine softened

2 cups sugar

2 cups brown sugar

4 large eggs

4 cups flour

2 teaspoons baking soda

1 teaspoon baking powder

1 tablespoon of vanilla, brandy or Grand Marnier

4 cups oatmeal (not quick oats)

4 cups smashed cereal

12 oz bag of chocolate chips

big handful of raisins

12 oz chopped dates

12 oz bag of white chocolate chips

SUBMITTED BY:
Rick Sebak - adapted from his mother's recipe

Rock Cookies

DIRECTIONS

Combine all ingredients; drop by teaspoon on cookie sheet. Bake at 350 degrees until light brown - about 10 to 12 minutes.

INGREDIENTS

1 cup shortening

1 cup sugar

4 eggs

1 box raisins

1 cup walnuts, cut in pieces

1 teaspoon vanilla

4 cups flour

1 teaspoon baking soda dissolved in 3 tablespoon

boiling water

SUBMITTED BY:

Jean Batovich, Nanty-Glo

Savina's Lace Cookies

DIRECTIONS

Preheat oven to 350 degrees. Line the baking sheets with foil. Sift flour, salt and baking powder together. Combine butter, sugar, eggs, vanilla and oatmeal, add flour. Drop by the 1/2 teaspoon on baking sheets, about 2 or 3 inches apart. Bake for 5 to 6 minutes or until golden brown. Cool completely. Yields 15 to 20 dozen depending upon size.

INGREDIENTS

4 tablespoons flour

1/2 teaspoon salt

1/2 teaspoon baking powder

1 cup (2 sticks) butter, melted

2 cups sugar

2 eggs, beaten

1/2 teaspoon vanilla extract

2 cups oatmeal

NOTES

This cookie mixture is easier to handle if it is refrigerated a few hours before baking.

SUBMITTED BY:
Virginia Luckhardt, Pittsburgh

Snowballs

Directions

Preheat oven to 350 degrees; grease baking sheets. In a bowl, combine butter, flour, sugar, vanilla, walnuts and a pinch of salt; mix until a stiff dough is formed. Shape into 1-inch balls and place on prepared sheets. Bake for 15 minutes. Roll in powdered sugar while still warm, and again when they are cool.

Ingredients

1 cup (2 sticks) butter, melted
2 cups flour
3 tablespoons sugar
2 teaspoons vanilla
1 cup ground walnuts
pinch of salt
powdered sugar for rolling

Submitted by:
Marion Cianciotti, Grapeville

35

Toasted Oatmeal Cookies

DIRECTIONS

In large skillet over medium heat, melt butter until lightly browned. Add oats, stirring constantly until golden, about 8-10 minutes. Remove from heat and cool. Preheat oven to 375 degrees. In large bowl, beat brown sugar, eggs and vanilla until light. Stir in flour, baking soda and peanuts until well blended. Let stand for 15 minutes. Drop by teaspoon onto greased cookie sheet. Bake at 375 degrees for 10 minutes or until golden; cool on rack. Yield 3 1/2 dozen. Keep stored in airtight container.

INGREDIENTS

3/4 cup butter or margarine

2 1/2 cups rolled oats

1 cup packed brown sugar

2 eggs, beaten

1 teaspoon vanilla

3/4 cup flour

1 teaspoon baking soda

1/2 cup salted peanuts, coarsely chopped

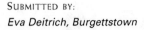

Walnut Crispies

DIRECTIONS

Preheat oven to 350 degrees. Cream butter and sugar. Sift together flour, salt, and baking soda. Add to butter mixture with nuts; mix well. Drop from a teaspoon onto greased cookie sheet. Bake in 350 degree oven for about 15 minutes. Makes 5 dozen.

INGREDIENTS

1 cup butter or margarine

2 1/2 cups brown sugar, packed

2 1/2 cups flour

1/4 teaspoon salt

1/2 teaspoon baking soda

1 cup chopped walnuts

SUBMITTED BY:

Charlotte Hogel, Pittsburgh

World's Most Famous Chocolate Chip Cookies

DIRECTIONS

Preheat oven to 375 degrees. Mix the margarine, sugars, eggs and vanilla until light and fluffy. In a separate bowl, mix flour, oatmeal, salt, baking powder, chocolate bar and baking soda together. Add to the creamed mixture; stir in the chocolate chips. Roll the dough into ping-pong-size balls and bake for 8 to 10 minutes. Do not over bake. Makes 8 to 9 dozen.

INGREDIENTS

2 cups margarine, softened

2 cups granulated sugar

2 cups brown sugar

4 eggs

2 teaspoons vanilla extract

4 cups flour

5 cups oatmeal, powdered

8 oz bar chocolate, finely grated

1 teaspoon salt

2 teaspoons baking soda

2 teaspoons baking powder

24 oz bag chocolate chips

SUBMITTED BY:
Jerry M. Rate, Pittsburgh

Bar Cookies

Apricot Bars

DIRECTIONS

Preheat oven to 350 degrees. Mix nuts, brown sugar and vanilla to make nut filling; set aside. Sift flour, sugar, salt and baking soda together, cut in shortening. Mix together beaten egg yolks, sour cream, vanilla and add all at once to flour mixture, stirring until dough forms a ball. Divide dough into three parts. Fit first third of dough onto greased cookie sheet that is 11x17 inches. Cover with nut filling. Roll out second third of dough and place over first layer. Cover this layer of dough with apricot filling. Roll out last third of dough and cut into lattice strips. Place on top of fruit filling in diagonal and horizontal design. Bake for 30-35 minutes at 350 degrees. Cool in pan; cut into diamond-shaped bars.

INGREDIENTS

Nut Filling:

3 cups ground nuts

1/2 cup brown sugar

1 teaspoon vanilla

Bars:

5 cups flour

1 cup sugar

1/2 teaspoon salt

4 teaspoons baking soda

1 cup plus 2 tablespoons shortening

4 egg yolks, beaten

1/2 pint sour cream

1 teaspoon vanilla

Apricot filling:

2 10 oz jars apricot filling

SUBMITTED BY:
Gloria Liscio, Pittsburgh

Butter Nut Chewies

DIRECTIONS

Preheat oven to 350 degrees. Grease a 9X13 pan. Beat eggs until light and foamy with an electric mixer. Beat in sugar, vanilla and margarine until creamy. Combine flour with baking powder and salt. Add to egg mixture. Mix at low speed until blended. Stir in nuts. Mixture will be stiff. Spread evenly in prepared pan. Bake at 350 degrees for 25 to 30 minutes. Cut into bars. Makes 2 dozen.

INGREDIENTS

2 eggs

2 cups firmly packed brown sugar

1 teaspoon vanilla

1/2 cup margarine, melted

1 1/2 cups flour

2 teaspoons baking powder

1/2 teaspoon salt

1 cup finely chopped nuts

SUBMITTED BY:
Patricia Kralik, Johnstown

America's
HOME COOKING

Candy Cookies

DIRECTIONS

Blend butter and peanut butter in a large bowl. Work in sugar and graham cracker crumbs with a wooden spoon until thoroughly combined. Press mixture evenly into a 13x9-inch baking pan. Boil water in a double boiler. Melt chocolate pieces in top of the double boiler. Quickly spread over top of cookies. Place in refrigerator and chill until firm. Cut into small squares.

INGREDIENTS

1 cup (2 sticks) butter or margarine, softened

1 cup crunchy peanut butter

1 pound box powdered sugar

1 1/2 cups graham cracker crumbs

6 oz package semisweet chocolate pieces

SUBMITTED BY:
Ellie Diulus, Penn Hills

Caramel Nut Crunch

DIRECTIONS

Lay the graham crackers flat, side by side, on the bottom of a jellyroll type cookie sheet. Cover the bottom of the cookie sheet completely, breaking graham crackers if necessary. In a heavy saucepan, combine the sugar and butter. Bring to a boil and cook for 5 minutes, stirring constantly with a wire whip. Immediately pour over the graham crackers; spread to coat. Sprinkle with chocolate chips. Let chips stand 1 minute to soften and then spread chocolate evenly with a spatula. Sprinkle with chipped nuts. Cool; break into pieces.

INGREDIENTS

10 to 12 whole graham crackers

3/4 cup firmly packed brown sugar

3/4 cup (1 1/2 sticks) sweet butter, not margarine

1 cup semi-sweet or milk chocolate chips

chopped nuts

SUBMITTED BY:
Sue K. Raynak, McKeesport

43

Carrot Bars with Cinnamon Cream Frosting

DIRECTIONS

Preheat oven to 375 degrees. Combine butter and water in a small saucepan and heat long enough to melt butter. Remove from heat and cool slightly.

In a large mixing bowl, stir together the flour, sugar, cinnamon, baking soda, salt, nutmeg and ginger. Add the butter mixture, egg, buttermilk and vanilla. Mix until well combined and then fold in the carrots, raisins and walnuts.

Pour into a greased 9x13 inch pan and bake at 375 for about 20-25 minutes. Cool and Frost. Makes about 30-34 bars.

Frosting: Beat together cream cheese, butter, vanilla and cinnamon until light and fluffy. Gradually beat in powdered sugar until smooth.

INGREDIENTS

1/3 cup butter

1/4 cup water

1 cup all purpose flour

1 cup sugar

1 teaspoon ground cinnamon

1/2 teaspoon baking soda

1/4 teaspoon salt

1/4 teaspoon ground nutmeg

1/4 teaspoon ground ginger

1 slightly beaten egg

1/4 cup buttermilk

1/2 teaspoon vanilla

1 cup shredded carrots

1/2 cup raisins

1/4 cup finely chopped walnuts

Frosting:

3 oz package of cream cheese

1/4 cup butter

1 teaspoon vanilla

1/4 teaspoon cinnamon

2 cups powdered sugar, sifted

SUBMITTED BY:
Antoinette Jucha

Coconut-Almond Bars

DIRECTIONS

Preheat oven to 350 degrees. Grease 15x10 inch jelly roll pan. In large bowl beat egg whites until soft peaks form. Gradually add sugar; beat until stiff peaks form - about 7 minutes. Add water, almond extract and vanilla; blend well. Stir in flour and coconut; mix well. Spread in greased pan. Arrange almonds over top of bars in 8 rows of 6 each. Bake at 350 degrees for 15-20 minutes or until lightly browned and top springs back when lightly touched in center. Cover pan with foil until cool. In small saucepan, melt chocolate chips and margarine over low heat, stirring occasionally. Drizzle over cooled bars. Cut into 48 bars.

INGREDIENTS

4 egg whites

1 1/2 cups sugar

1 tablespoon water

1 teaspoon almond extract

2 teaspoons vanilla

1 cup flour

3 cups shredded coconut

48 whole almonds

1/2 cup semi-sweet chocolate chips

3 tablespoons margarine

SUBMITTED BY:
LuAnne Salak, New Castle

Date Nut Bars

DIRECTIONS

Preheat oven to 350 degrees. Cream eggs, sugar, butter and water well. Combine flour, salt and baking powder and add to creamed mixture. Fold in dates and nuts; add a small amount of flour to keep dates from sticking together. Put into greased and floured 6 1/2 X 10 inch pan; smooth out. Bake at 350 degrees 20-30 minutes. Sprinkle with powdered sugar when done.

INGREDIENTS

2 eggs

1 cup sugar

1 tablespoon butter

1 tablespoon water

1 cup flour

1/2 teaspoon salt

1/2 teaspoon baking powder

2 cups chopped dates

1 cup chopped nuts

Powdered sugar

SUBMITTED BY:
Dorothy J. Shaner, Stoneboro

Fruit Bars

Directions

Preheat oven to 350 degrees. Cream the butter, brown sugar, egg, molasses and milk. Combine flour, baking soda, salt and baking powder and add to creamed mixture. Fold in fruit and nuts; blend well. Put in greased and floured 13x9 inch pan. Bake at 350 degrees 25-30 minutes. Cool on wire rack. Cut into 48 bars and store in an air tight container.

Ingredients

1/4 cup butter or oleo, softened

1/3 cup light brown sugar

1 large egg

1/2 cup molasses

1/2 cup milk

2 cups flour

1 1/2 teaspoons baking soda

1/4 teaspoon salt

1/4 teaspoon baking powder

1/4 cup seedless dark raisins

3/4 cup chopped dates

1/4 cup chopped maraschino cherries

3/4 cup chopped walnuts or pecans, optional

Submitted by:
Dorothy J. Shaner, Stoneboro

47

Garden Fresh Dessert Bars

DIRECTIONS

Preheat oven to 350 degrees. In a large bowl, combine eggs, sugar, oil, lemon juice and lemon peel. Beat by hand until well blended. Add zucchini and mix well. Sift flour, baking soda, baking powder and salt together. Stir dry ingredients into zucchini mixture and fold in nuts. Pour into greased 9x13 inch baking pan. Bake at 350 degrees for 45-50 minutes. Cool, cut into squares and sprinkle with powdered sugar.

INGREDIENTS

3 eggs

1 1/4 cups sugar

1 cup oil

1/4 cup freshly squeezed lemon juice

2 teaspoons grated lemon peel

2 cups finely shredded unpeeled zucchini

2 cups flour

2 teaspoons baking soda

1/4 teaspoon baking powder

1 teaspoon salt

1 cup coarsely chopped nuts

Powdered sugar

SUBMITTED BY:

Lucille Tanner, New Castle

Iced Applesauce Bars

DIRECTIONS

Preheat oven to 350 degrees. In a medium mixing bowl with electric mixer on high speed, beat dry gingerbread mix and applesauce for 2 minutes. Add raisins, lemon peel and nuts; stir to combine. Spread mixture evenly in greased and flour 13x9 inch pan. Bake in preheated 350 degree oven for 25-30 minutes or until center springs back when lightly pressed. Let cool completely in pan on wire rack.

Icing: Blend powdered sugar, milk and lemon juice in a small bowl, stirring until smooth. Drizzle icing over baked layer in pan. Let stand until icing is set. Cut into bars, remove from pan and store in an airtight container to enhance flavor.

INGREDIENTS

14 oz package gingerbread mix
3/4 cup applesauce
1 cup raisins
2 teaspoons grated lemon peel
1/2 cup nuts, optional

Icing
1 1/2 cup powdered sugar
1 to 2 tablespoons milk
1 to 2 tablespoons lemon juice

SUBMITTED BY:
Beni Downing, Penn Hills

Lemon Bars

DIRECTIONS

Preheat oven to 350 degrees. Mix butter,
flour and powdered sugar and press into a
9x13 inch pan. Bake at 350 degrees for 20 minutes. Combine remaining ingredients and pour
over crust. Bake for 25 minutes at 350 degrees.
Dust top with powdered sugar. Cool before
cutting into squares.

INGREDIENTS

1 cup (2 sticks) butter (not
margarine), melted

2 cups flour

1/2 cup powdered sugar

4 eggs, slightly beaten

2 cups sugar

4 tablespoons flour

1/2 teaspoon baking powder

6 tablespoons lemon juice

SUBMITTED BY:

Mrs. Ernest Lucini, Beaver Falls

Oatmeal Caramel Cookies

DIRECTIONS

Preheat oven to 350 degrees. Melt together caramels and evaporated milk. Cool slightly. Combine flour, oats, brown sugar, salt, soda, butter. Press half of flour mixture into a greased 9x13 pan. Bake 10 minutes at 350 degrees. Remove from oven, sprinkle on chips and pecans. Spread caramel mixture over this. Sprinkle with remaining flour mixture. Bake 15 to 20 minutes. Chill 1 or 2 hours - cut into bars.

INGREDIENTS

50 light caramels

1/2 cup evaporated milk

2 cups flour

2 cups quick rolled oats

1 1/2 cups brown sugar

1/2 teaspoon salt

1 teaspoon soda

1 cup melted butter

6 oz chocolate chips

1 cup chopped pecans

NOTE

You can use walnuts instead of pecans. Be careful not to over bake, check after baking 15 minutes.

SUBMITTED BY:
Frances Sbarro, Wampum

Old World Raspberry Bars

DIRECTIONS

Preheat oven to 350 degrees. Mix butter and sugar together. Add flour and nuts. Blend well. Add eggs one at a time and beat until blended. Grease 15x10 inch jelly roll pan. Press a little more than half of the mixture into the bottom of the pan. Spread raspberry filing to within a half an inch of all sides. Crumble remaining dough on top. Bake for about 45-50 minutes at 350 degrees. Cut into squares or bars when completely cool.

INGREDIENTS

4 1/2 cups flour

2 cups sugar

2 cups butter

2 cups chopped nuts

2 eggs

2 cups raspberry filling

SUBMITTED BY:
Maria Merante

Peanut Cookies

DIRECTIONS

Preheat oven to 350 degrees. Combine all dough ingredients except marshmallows; mix. Press in 9x13 inch pan. Bake 15 minutes or until light brown. Remove from oven and immediately sprinkle with marshmallows. Return to oven 2 minutes until they start to puff.

Topping: In large saucepan, heat Karo, chips, oleo, and vanilla until chips are melted. Be sure it is smooth then remove from heat; add cereal and peanuts. Spoon into pan immediately while topping is still warm. Spread to cover. Chill and cut into bars.

INGREDIENTS

1 1/2 cups flour
1/2 teaspoon salt
1 teaspoon vanilla
2/3 cup brown sugar
1/2 cup oleo
1/2 teaspoon baking powder
2 egg yolks
1/4 teaspoon baking soda
3 cups mini-marshmallows

Topping:
2/3 cup white Karo syrup
12 oz peanut butter chips
1/4 cup oleo
2 teaspoons vanilla
2 cups Rice Krispies
2 cups cocktail peanuts

SUBMITTED BY:
Alice Fucaro, New Castle

53

Poor Man's Bar Cookies

DIRECTIONS

Preheat oven to 350 degrees. Cook raisins with water for 10 minutes. After 10 minutes, some water will boil away. Measure water and add more to equal 1 cup. Put shortening in hot mixture so it melts. Cream sugar, egg, cloves and cinnamon. Add to raisin mixture with nuts. Sift together flour, salt and baking soda. Add to raisin mixture. Spread into a greased and floured 15x10 inch jelly roll pan. Bake in 350 degree oven for 25 or 30 minutes until raised and done when you test with cake tester. Cool and ice with butter cream glaze.

Glaze: Combine all ingredients with enough water to make a thin glaze. Spread over sheet of cookies. Cool and let glaze set. Cut into bars and serve. Makes 3-4 dozen.

INGREDIENTS

1 cup dark raisins

1 cup water

1/2 cup margarine or shortening

1 cup granulated sugar

1 egg

1/2 teaspoon ground cloves

1 teaspoon cinnamon

1 cup chopped walnuts

2 cups flour

1/2 teaspoon salt

1 teaspoon baking soda

Butter Cream Glaze:

2 cups sifted powdered sugar

2-4 tablespoons margarine

1 teaspoon vanilla

water

SUBMITTED BY:

Norma Oskin, Duquesne

America's
HOME COOKING

Raisin Cookies

DIRECTIONS

Cream together brown sugar and lard or shortening; add eggs and ground raisins. Sift together flour, cinnamon, nutmeg and cloves. Dissolve the baking soda into the milk, and add alternately with the flour. Refrigerate dough for 1/2 hour.

Preheat oven to 350 degrees. Roll out dough on a floured board until about 1/4 to 1/2 inch thick. Bake for 12 to 15 minutes, until just slightly brown. Cool; sprinkle with powdered sugar.

INGREDIENTS

2 cups brown sugar

1 cup lard or shortening

3 eggs

1 pound raisins, ground

5 cups flour

1 teaspoon cinnamon

1 teaspoon nutmeg

1/2 teaspoon cloves

1 teaspoon baking soda

1/2 cup sour milk or buttermilk

powdered sugar

SUBMITTED BY:
Ethelclaire Smith, Smithton

Scotch Shortbread

DIRECTIONS

Preheat oven to 300 degrees. Cream the sugar and butter together. Sift flour with baking powder and salt. Add to butter mixture. Press dough into ungreased jelly roll pan and prick with the tines of a fork. Bake 30-40 minutes at 300 degrees or until delicately brown. Cut in pan while warm. These cookies freeze well.

INGREDIENTS

1 cup sugar

2 cups butter, softened
(do not substitute margarine)

4 cups all-purpose flour

1/2 teaspoon baking powder

1/2 teaspoon salt

SUBMITTED BY:
Eve Roha, Greensburg

Seven-Layer Cookies

DIRECTIONS

Preheat oven to 350 degrees, 325 degrees if using a glass dish. In 9x13 inch baking pan, melt margarine in oven, then remove. Sprinkle graham cracker crumbs over melted butter. Mix together and press into bottom of pan. Pour half of sweetened condensed milk evenly over crumbs. Sprinkle coconut over milk then sprinkle chocolate chips over the coconut. Sprinkle butterscotch chips over the chocolate chips then drizzle the remaining milk evenly over the butterscotch chips. Sprinkle with nuts to cover. Bake for 25-30 minutes or until lightly browned. Loosen sides from pan immediately after removing from the oven. Allow to cool completely before cutting into squares. Store loosely covered at room temperature.

INGREDIENTS

1/2 cup butter or margarine

1 1/2 cups graham cracker crumbs

14 oz can sweetened condensed milk

1 1/4 cups flaked coconut

6 oz package chocolate chips

6 oz package butterscotch chips

1 1/2 cups chopped nuts

SUBMITTED BY:
Cherri Williams, Pittsburgh

TJ Finger Cookies

DIRECTIONS

Preheat oven to 350 degrees. In a heavy three-quart saucepan, dissolve the sugar in the butter and bring to a boil. While the sugar and butter are cooking, line a 9x13 inch jellyroll pan with aluminum foil and spray with nonstick. Completely cover the bottom of the pan with a layer of saltines. Cook the butter mixture for two minutes, and remove from the heat. Add the vanilla. Carefully pour this mixture over the crackers, trying to moisten them all. Place in the oven for 10 minutes.

Remove the tray from oven and sprinkle with the chocolate morsels. Wait a minute for the chocolate to soften and then spread evenly with a spatula. Sprinkle with the chopped nuts and refrigerate until firm.

Remove from the pan and peel away the aluminum foil. Break into pieces and store in an airtight container. (Or eat immediately!)

INGREDIENTS

1/2 cup sugar

1 cup (2 sticks) butter

saltine crackers

1 teaspoon vanilla extract

12 oz chocolate morsels

1 cup toasted chopped nuts

SUBMITTED BY:
Chris Fennimore, WQED Pittsburgh

Turtle Bars

DIRECTIONS

Preheat oven to 350 degrees. Place cake mix, butter and 1/3 cup evaporated milk in large mixer bowl; beat at high speed until well mixed. Set aside remaining milk. Place half of cake mix mixture in greased 9x13 inch pan and press into bottom. Bake at 350 degrees for 6 minutes. Remove from oven and cool to room temperature.

Unwrap caramels and place in heavy saucepan with remaining 1/3 cup of milk. Stir over medium heat until smooth. Pour evenly over cooled cake mixture in pan. Sprinkle with chocolate chips and nuts. Take pieces of the remaining uncooked cake mix mixture and press them into even thickness with your hands. Lay them on top of nuts, covering the entire surface. Bake in 350 degree oven for 15-18 minutes or until the surface is no longer glossy. Cool in pan on rack then cut into small bars.

INGREDIENTS

1 box (18.5 oz) deluxe Swiss chocolate cake mix (can be substituted)

1/2 cup butter, melted

2/3 cup evaporated milk, divided

14 oz individually wrapped light caramels

12 oz package semisweet chocolate chips

1 cup coarsely chopped pecans

SUBMITTED BY:
Eve Roha, Greensburg

America's
HOME COOKING

Ethnic Favorites

Anise Cookies

DIRECTIONS

Cookies: Preheat oven to 350 degrees. In a large bowl, cream the shortening and sugar until light and fluffy. Add the eggs, one at a time, beating well after each addition. Beat in the anise extract. Gradually add flour, baking powder and salt. Place the dough on a well-floured surface. Knead the dough and add flour so the dough is not sticky. Do not add too much flour or the cookies will be dry. Divide the dough in three, forming loaves that measure 12x2 1/2 inches.

Bake the cookies for 20 to 25 minutes or until lightly brown. Cool on a cookie sheet; slice loaves into 1/2-inch thick pieces when cool. Frost with pastry brush and sprinkle on the candy while the frosting is still soft.

Frosting: In a small saucepan, warm the milk. Add the sugar and mix until smooth. Add the anise extract. The frosting should be smooth and easy to spread on the cookies. If the frosting becomes too thick, add a little milk.

INGREDIENTS

2/3 cup shortening

1 cup sugar

6 eggs

1 tablespoon anise extract

4 cups flour

2 tablespoons baking powder

1 teaspoon salt

Frosting:

1 tablespoon warm milk

2 cups powdered sugar, sifted

1 teaspoon anise extract

colored candy sprinkles

SUBMITTED BY:

Christine Pellegrini, Chicora

61

Biscotti in a Pan

DIRECTIONS

Preheat oven to 350 degrees. Blend together butter and sugar. Beat in eggs one at a time. Add extracts. Stir in flour and baking powder. Stir in nuts just to blend. Pour batter and spread evenly into greased jelly roll pan. Bake for about 25 minutes. Cut into slices when cool and toast if desired.

INGREDIENTS

5 eggs

1 1/2 cups sugar

1 cup melted butter

1 teaspoon vanilla

2 teaspoons flavored extract (for example: anise, almond, lemon)

2 cups flour

1 teaspoon baking powder

3/4 cup toasted ground almonds, if desired

SUBMITTED BY:
Maria Merante

Biscotti
(Italian Anise Slices)

DIRECTIONS

Preheat oven to 350 degrees; lightly grease baking sheets. Sift flour, baking powder and salt in large bowl. Cream butter, sugar and extracts; beat in eggs one at a time. Add flour mixture and almonds. Turn out on floured board and knead gently. If dough is sticky, put in refrigerator for at least one hour. Shape into three loaves. Put on the baking sheet and cook until firm, about 25 minutes. Remove from oven and let cool slightly. While still warm, cut in 1/2-inch slices (electric knife works well). Heat oven to 400 degrees then turn off. Place slices cut side down on cookie sheet and bake until toasted and dried out, about 10 to 20 minutes. Turn once.

INGREDIENTS

6 cups flour

6 teaspoons baking powder

1/2 teaspoon salt

1 cup (2 sticks) butter

1 1/2 cups sugar

2 teaspoons anise extract
or 1/2 teaspoon anise oil

2 teaspoons lemon extract

1 teaspoon vanilla extract

6 eggs

1 cup finely chopped almonds, toasted

SUBMITTED BY:
Lorraine Troiano, Vandergrift

Chinese Almond Cookies

DIRECTIONS

Preheat the oven to 375 degrees. Cream shortening, sugar, egg and almond extract. Combine flour, ground nuts and salt; add to mix. Shape into 1 1/2 - 2 inch balls. Place on ungreased cookie sheet and place whole almond in center of each cookie. Brush with egg yolk and water mixture. Bake at 375 degrees for 12 minutes.

INGREDIENTS

1 cup shortening

1 cup sugar

1 egg

1 1/2 teaspoons almond extract

2 cups flour

1/2 cup ground almonds

1/2 teaspoon salt

whole blanched almonds for garnish

1 egg yolk

1 teaspoon water

SUBMITTED BY:
Marilyn Rollin and Amy Rollin, Pittsburgh

Chinese Almond Pizelles

DIRECTIONS

Preheat pizelle maker. Sift together flour, baking powder, granulated sugar and almonds; set aside. Cream butter and sugar. Add eggs one at a time and beat until light. Add almond extract and flour mixture. Drop by spoonful onto preheated pizelle maker. Bake as directed for pizelles.

INGREDIENTS

3 cups flour

1 teaspoon baking powder

1 3/4 cups granulated sugar

1/3 cup ground or finely chopped almonds

1 cup (2 sticks) of butter

2 eggs

1 teaspoon almond extract

SUBMITTED BY:
Honey Kolsun, Windgap

Chocolate Macadamia Nut Biscotti

DIRECTIONS

Partially fill a saucepan with water; bring to a simmer. Combine chocolate and butter in a small heatproof bowl; set over the water until ingredients soften. Remove from the heat and stir until smooth. Let cool. Sift together the flour, cocoa powder, baking powder and salt onto a large piece of waxed paper. In a large mixing bowl, beat eggs until foamy. Add sugars, liqueur, rum and vanilla and beat smooth. Stir in cooled chocolate. Add flour mixture and stir until well combined. Add coconut and nuts. Cover and refrigerate for one hour. Preheat oven to 300 degrees. Butter and flour a large baking pan. Divide dough into four pieces, shaping each piece into a log measuring 8x1 3/4 inches. Arrange logs on prepared baking sheet about 2 inches apart. Brush with egg white and bake for 50 minutes. Slide logs onto rack to cool completely. Cut each log into 1/2-inch slices on the diagonal. Place slices cut side down on baking sheet and continue baking for 15 to 20 minutes, or until lightly toasted. Makes about 52 biscotti.

INGREDIENTS

5 oz semi-sweet baking chocolate

6 tablespoons unsalted butter

1/2 pound all-purpose flour

1 cup unsweetened cocoa powder

2 teaspoons baking powder

1 teaspoon salt

3 large eggs

1/2 cup granulated sugar

1/2 cup brown sugar

1/4 cup coffee liqueur

1 tablespoon dark rum

1 teaspoon vanilla extract

1 cup lightly packed shredded coconut

1 cup unsalted macadamia nuts, chopped

1 egg white, lightly beaten

SUBMITTED BY:
Patricia E. McCaughtry, Pittsburgh

Chrustyky
(Angels' Wings)

DIRECTIONS

Beat egg yolks until pale yellow. Combine eggs with flour, sugar and salt in large bowl. Mix until well blended. Blend in sour cream, butter, vanilla and almond extract. Knead mixture to form large ball. Roll out on floured board to 1/8-inch thickness. Cut dough into strips 2 inches wide. Cut strips diagonally to form 3-inch diamond shapes. Make a slit in center of each, and insert one point of diamond into slit and pull it through. Heat oil to 375 degrees. Fry cookies for 3 minutes, until lightly browned on all sides. Drain on heavy paper. Sprinkle with confectioner's sugar. Makes 9 dozen.

INGREDIENTS

6 egg yolks

4 cups all-purpose flour, sifted

2 tablespoons sugar

1/4 teaspoon salt

1 cup sour cream

2 tablespoons butter or margarine

1 teaspoon vanilla extract

1/2 teaspoon almond extract

oil for frying

powdered sugar for dusting

SUBMITTED BY:
Mary Hanczco, Carnegie

America's
HOME COOKING

Grandma Jones's Welsh Cookies

Directions

Mix together butter and sugars. Add eggs and milk; mix. Add remaining ingredients and mix well. Add enough flour to roll. Roll out the dough and cut in desired shapes. Heat some butter on a griddle; cook the cookies on it as you would pancakes.

Ingredients

1 cup butter

1 cup white sugar

1 cup brown sugar

2 eggs

1/2 cup milk

2 cups flour, plus more to reach consistency

1/2 teaspoon nutmeg

1/2 teaspoon cinnamon

1/2 teaspoon baking soda

3 teaspoons baking powder

1 teaspoon salt

1 tablespoon vinegar

1 cup currants or chopped raisins

Submitted by:
Olive Rhoads, Alliance

America's HOME COOKING

Greek Sesame Cookies (Koulourakia)

DIRECTIONS

Preheat oven to 350 degrees. In mixer, cream butter and sugar well. Add beaten egg, creaming well. Add baking powder and vanilla. Sift flour with baking soda, cinnamon, and salt. Gradually add flour to creamed mixture, one cup at a time, until dough is soft and not sticky. Remove bowl from mixer. Gradually add flour and knead well.

On lightly floured surface, roll 1 tablespoon of dough into a 6 inch long rope. Shape into circles or twists. Place on greased cookie sheet 1 inch apart. Sprinkle top with sesame seeds and brush with beaten eggs.

Bake at 350 degrees for 15-20 minutes until a light golden brown. Cool on wire rack. Makes about 60 cookies.

INGREDIENTS

1 pound (four sticks) unsalted butter

1 1/2 cups sugar

2 large egg yolks

1/2 teaspoon baking powder dissolved in 1/4 cup warm milk

2 teaspoons vanilla extract

1 teaspoon baking soda

1 teaspoon cinnamon

1/8 teaspoon salt

4 1/2 to 5 cups flour

Glaze:

2 eggs

sesame seeds

SUBMITTED BY:

Florence Hazimanolis

America's
HOME COOKING

Hazelnut-Black Pepper Biscotti

DIRECTIONS

Preheat oven to 350 degrees, lightly butter a baking sheet. Spread hazelnuts on a large baking sheet and toast for 10-12 minutes until golden brown. Transfer to a medium bowl to cool. Chop lightly. In a food processor, combine the flour, baking powder, salt and 2/3 cup of sugar. Add the butter and pulse until the mixture resembles coarse meal. Add the mixture to the hazelnuts and toss. Mix in the black pepper. Using a fork, lightly beat the eggs with the vanilla. Stir into the flour mixture; mix with your hands until just blended. Pat into a disk. Lightly butter the baking sheet. On a lightly floured work surface, quarter the disk. Using your hands, roll each wedge into an 8 inch log. Place the logs 2 inches apart on the prepared baking sheet and flatten with the heel of your hand to a width of 2 inches; sprinkle the tops with the remaining 1/2 teaspoon of sugar. Bake for about 20 minutes or until golden brown.

Using 2 metal spatulas, carefully transfer the logs to a rack to cool slightly - 5-10 minutes. Place the logs on a work surface. Using a sharp knife in a quick motion, slice each log on the diagonal 3/4 inch thick. Place the biscotti cut side down on the baking sheet and bake for 5-7 minutes, just until they begin to color. Transfer to a rack to cool completely.

INGREDIENTS

1 1/2 cups unsalted hazelnuts

1 3/4 cups all purpose flour

1/2 teaspoon baking powder

1/4 teaspoon salt

2/3 cup plus 1/2 teaspoon sugar

4 tablespoons cold unsalted butter, cut into small pieces

1 1/2 tablespoons black pepper

2 large eggs

1/2 teaspoon pure vanilla extract

SUBMITTED BY:
Theresa M. Falvo, Pittsburgh

America's
HOME COOKING

Holiday Macaroons

DIRECTIONS

Preheat oven to 325 degrees. Beat eggs, add sugar. Beat mixture until thick, about 5 minutes. Sift together flour, baking powder and salt. Combine with egg mixture. Stir in margarine, vanilla and coconut. Grease and flour cookie sheets. Drop by teaspoon no larger than a quarter or the cookies will spread too much. Bake at 325 degrees for 10-13 minutes until delicately browned.

INGREDIENTS

4 eggs

1 1/2 cups sugar

2/3 cup flour

1/2 teaspoon baking powder

1/4 teaspoon salt

2 tablespoons margarine, melted and cooled

1 teaspoon vanilla

5 cups flaked coconut

1 jar maraschino cherries (optional- see note)

NOTES

Before baking you may top each cookie with 1/2 maraschino cherry. To prepare cherries, drain and gently pat dry with a paper towel. If cherries are frozen, they cut in half more neatly and the color doesn't bleed onto the macaroons.

SUBMITTED BY:
Susan R. Tenney, Mather

Honey Spice Cookies

DIRECTIONS

Preheat oven to 325 degrees. Cream together margarine, oil and sugar until light and fluffy. Beat in yolk, orange juice and lemon juice. In a separate bowl, stir flour, baking powder and cinnamon; add to creamed mixture alternately with milk, beating well with each addition. Place one-tablespoon drops of dough on a cookie sheet; bake for 25 minutes. Cool cookies on wire rack, making sure to place wax paper under rack. After making the Honey Syrup, bathe the cookies in it. Roll the tops in nuts; cool and drain cookies on the rack. Makes about 30 cookies.

Honey Syrup: In a saucepan, combine all ingredients. Bring to boiling; boil gently uncovered for 10 minutes. Remove from heat and keep warm.

INGREDIENTS

1/2 cup margarine, softened

1/4 cup salad oil

1/4 cup sugar

1 egg yolk

2 tablespoons orange juice

1 tablespoon lemon juice

2 1/4 cups all purpose flour

3/4 teaspoon baking powder

1/4 teaspoon ground cinnamon

1/4 cup milk

1 1/2 cups toasted chopped walnuts

Honey Syrup:

1 cup sugar

1/2 cup water

1/2 cup honey

SUBMITTED BY:
Vivienne M. Cotchen, Johnstown

72

America's
HOME COOKING

Italian Chocolate Spice Cookies

DIRECTIONS

Preheat oven to 350 degrees; slightly grease baking sheets. In a large bowl mix together the flour, cocoa, baking powder, sugar, cloves, all-spice and cinnamon. Add milk, margarine, vanilla and chopped nuts. Roll in balls onto the baking sheet. Bake for 10 to 12 minutes. Roll in powdered sugar.

INGREDIENTS

8 cups flour

1 cup cocoa

8 teaspoons baking powder

3 cups sugar

1 teaspoon cloves

2 teaspoons allspice

4 teaspoons cinnamon

3 cups milk

1 pound (4 sticks) margarine, melted

1 teaspoon vanilla extract

1 pound chopped nuts

powdered sugar for rolling

SUBMITTED BY:
Mrs. Stanley Paulovich, Monaca

Italian Lemon Drop Cookies

DIRECTIONS

Cookies: Preheat oven to 400 degrees; grease cookie sheets. Beat eggs for 10 minutes. Add sugar, oil, vanilla, lemon juice and rind and beat 5 more minutes. Add baking powder and fold in flour a little at a time. Drop by heaping teaspoonful on sheet. Bake for 10 minutes.

Frosting: Combine powdered sugar, lemon extract and water to desired consistency. Mix well and spoon frosting on cookies.

INGREDIENTS

Cookies:

12 eggs

2 cups oil

2 cups sugar

1 teaspoon vanilla extract

1 lemon, juice and rind

5 teaspoons baking powder

5 cups flour

Frosting:

2 (1 pound.) boxes powdered sugar

2 teaspoons lemon extract

2 teaspoons water

SUBMITTED BY:
Mrs. William Roth, Farrell

74

Kolacke Cookies

DIRECTIONS

Preheat oven to 350 degrees. In 1 quart saucepan, heat milk until it just comes to a boil; let cool until warm. Dissolve yeast in warm milk. Meanwhile, in a large mixer bowl, cut butter into chunks. Add flour, sugar and salt. Beat at low speed, scraping bowl often until mixture resembles coarse crumbs. Stir egg and vanilla into milk mixture. Add milk mixture to flour mixture; beat at low speed, scraping bowl often until well mixed. Divide dough in half. On lightly floured surface roll out dough, half at a time, to an 1/8" to 1/4" thickness. Cut dough into 3 inch squares. Place 1 teaspoon preserves on each square. Bring up 2 opposite corners or each square to center; pinch tightly to hold together. Place on greased cookie sheet and brush with beaten egg. Bake 10-14 minutes or until golden brown. Remove from cookie sheets immediately and cool completely.

Glaze: In small bowl, stir together all glaze ingredients until smooth. Drizzle over cookies.

INGREDIENTS

1/2 cup milk

1 package active dry yeast

1 cup butter, cold

3 cups flour

1/4 cup sugar

1/2 teaspoon salt

1 egg

1 teaspoon vanilla

1/2 cup preserves, any flavor

1 egg, well-beaten

Glaze:

2/3 cup powdered sugar

2-3 teaspoons milk

1 teaspoon almond extract

SUBMITTED BY:
Carleen Sisler, Mather

Lee's Sesame Seed Cookies

Directions

Preheat oven to 350 degrees. Mix flour, baking powder and sugar; add shortening, eggs and vanilla. Mix well. Roll small handfuls of dough on a floured board into a thin roll about the size of a pencil. Cut into 3-inch segments. Roll into sesame seeds to cover dough. Place on cookie sheet one inch apart. Bake until lightly browned. Makes about 8 dozen.

Ingredients

3 cups flour

1 teaspoon baking powder

1 1/4 cups sugar

1 cup shortening

3 eggs

1 teaspoon vanilla extract

2 cups (approximately) sesame seeds

Notes

These cookies freeze and travel well.

Submitted by:
Barbara Ryan, Pittsburgh

America's HOME COOKING

Mildred Halechko's Amaretto Medallions

DIRECTIONS

Preheat oven to 325 degrees. Cover cookie sheet with baking parchment. Remove 48 slivered almond pieces and reserve. Chop remaining almonds in blender or food processor; measure 1/2 cup and set aside. In smaller bowl combine shortening and brown sugar, mix well. Add beaten egg and liqueur, beat well. Combine flour, salt and baking soda; gradually add to egg mixture. Stir in 1/2 cup chopped almonds. Drop by teaspoon on cookie sheet and press slivered almond piece on top of each cookie. Bake 8-9 minutes until edges are light brown. Do not overbake. Remove medallions carefully from baking sheet and cool on rack; store in ceramic container. Makes about 4 dozen small cookies.

INGREDIENTS

4 oz slivered almonds

1/2 cup butter-flavored shortening - (do not substitute)

1 cup dark brown sugar

1 egg, beaten

2 tablespoons amaretto liqueur

1 cup all-purpose flour

1/2 teaspoon salt

1/2 teaspoon baking soda

SUBMITTED BY:
Mildred Halechko, Glenshaw

Nut Horns

DIRECTIONS

Scald milk and cool enough to dissolve yeast. Mix together margarine, sugar, flour and eggs; mix in yeast mixture and chill at least 2 hours or overnight.

Nut Filling: Combine the nuts and vanilla with enough of the evaporated milk to make a paste.

Preheat the oven to 450 degrees. Divide dough into 10 balls. Roll each ball, one at a time, into a flattened circle (like pie dough), on granulated sugar. Cut each circle of dough into 12 wedges. Place 1 teaspoon nut filling at large end and roll up. Bake at 450 degrees on an ungreased cookie sheet for 6 minutes or until they start to brown. Makes 10 dozen.

INGREDIENTS

1 cup milk

1/2 cup yeast cake (large size)

1 pound (4 sticks) margarine

3 cups sugar

6 cups flour

3 eggs

Nut Filling:

4 cups ground nuts

2 teaspoons vanilla extract
enough evaporated milk to make a paste

SUBMITTED BY:
Rose Boyd, Ford City

Orange Walnut Biscotti

DIRECTIONS

Preheat oven to 325 degrees. Sift dry ingredients together. Cream eggs, egg yolk, orange extract and butter together; add to dry ingredients. Form two logs and brush with egg white. Bake at 325 degrees for 30-40 minutes or until golden. Cool, slice diagonally and toast on a cookie sheet.

INGREDIENTS

3 2/3 cups flour

1 cup chopped walnuts

1 teaspoon baking powder

1/4 teaspoon baking soda

1 1/3 cup sugar

2 tablespoons lemon zest

2 tablespoons orange zest

2 whole eggs

1 yolk, save egg white

2 tablespoons orange extract

1/2 cup (1 stick) melted butter

SUBMITTED BY:
Joseph Certo

Pfefferneusse

DIRECTIONS

Preheat oven to 350 degrees. Combine flour, baking powder, lemon peel, salt, spices and pepper in a mixing bowl. In larger bowl, cream sugar and margarine; beat in egg. Add flour mixture alternating with milk, beating well after each addition. Roll into small balls or drop dough onto lightly greased cookie sheet. Bake at 350 degrees for 15-17 minutes. Cool slightly; roll in powdered sugar and cool completely. Yields 4-5 dozen .

INGREDIENTS

1 2/3 cups flour

1 1/2 teaspoons baking powder

1/2 teaspoon lemon peel, chopped

1/4 teaspoon salt

1/4 teaspoon cinnamon

1/4 teaspoon nutmeg

1/8 teaspoon ground cloves

1/2 teaspoon anise seed

1/8 teaspoon white pepper

1/3 cup softened margarine

1/2 cup sugar

1 egg

1/2 cup milk

Powdered sugar for rolling

SUBMITTED BY:
Susan R. Tenney, Mather

Pignolia Nut Cookies

DIRECTIONS

Crumble almond paste into mixer bowl. Sift the sugars together and gradually add to the almond paste a little at a time with part of the egg white. Very gradually add last amount of egg white. This mixture should be very stiff. With pastry bag and no tube, squeeze mounds the size of a quarter. Roll into nuts and make an oval cookie. Let stand at room temperature at least 4 hours or overnight.

Preheat oven to 300 degrees. Bake on cookie sheets lined with silicone paper or sprayed with cooking oil and dusted with flour for about 20 minutes or slightly golden. Store in tightly covered container in refrigerator.

INGREDIENTS

8 oz almond paste

1/2 cup sugar

1/2 cup powdered sugar

1/4 cup egg whites (about 2)

1 cup pignolia nuts

NOTES

These freeze very well in sealed plastic freezer bags.

SUBMITTED BY:
Theresa M. Falvo, Pittsburgh

81

Pizelle

DIRECTIONS

Beat eggs well, and add sugar gradually. Add shortening, oil and extracts, beating until smooth. Add flour and baking powder. Cover and let sit overnight in refrigerator. Heat pizelle iron for 10 minutes. Drop dough from a teaspoon on iron. Bake about 1 minute or until golden brown. Makes 10 to 11 dozen medium size pizelles.

INGREDIENTS

9 eggs

2 1/4 cups sugar

3/4 cup margarine, melted

3/4 cup oil

3 tablespoons vanilla extract

1 teaspoon anise extract

1 teaspoon orange extract

1 1/2 teaspoons orange rind

2 tablespoons baking powder

5 1/2 cups flour

SUBMITTED BY:
Lorraine Troiano, Vandergrift

Sour Cream Filled Hungarian Cookies

DIRECTIONS

Preheat oven to 350 degrees. Cream margarine, shortening, sugar and eggs. Add flour, baking powder, soda, salt, vanilla and sour cream. Beat - mixture will be very thick. Place one teaspoon of batter on a lightly greased cookie sheet. Press slightly with floured fingers. Add 1/2 teaspoon filling on top. Add 1/2 teaspoon batter on top of filling. Spread batter a little to cover filling. Repeat with remaining batter. Bake 12 - 15 minutes at 350 degrees until light brown on bottom. Drizzle with your favorite powdered sugar icing on top while hot. Sprinkle with nuts. Makes 6 dozen.

INGREDIENTS

1/2 cup margarine

1/2 cup shortening

1 cup sugar

2 eggs

3 3/4 cups flour

2 teaspoons baking powder

1 teaspoon baking soda

pinch salt

1 teaspoon vanilla

1/2 pint (1 cup) sour cream

apricot or cherry filling

powdered sugar icing

nuts

SUBMITTED BY:

Cornelia J. Salak, New Castle

Spiced Almond Cookies

DIRECTIONS

In a mixing bowl, cream butter and shortening; beat in sugars until light and fluffy. Add eggs and beat well. Combine dry ingredients and stir into creamed with mixture, along with almonds. Shape into three 9 by 1 1/2 inch rolls. Wrap in waxed paper and chill 2 to 3 days for spices to blend.

Preheat oven to 350 degrees. Cut rolls into 1/4 inch thick slices. Place on ungreased cookie sheet. Bake at 350 degrees for 12-14 minutes or until set. Remove cookies to a wire rack to cool. Yield 7 dozen.

INGREDIENTS

1 cup butter or margarine, softened

1/2 cup shortening

1 cup brown sugar, packed

1 cup sugar

2 eggs

4 cups all-purpose flour

1 teaspoon cinnamon

1 teaspoon baking soda

1 teaspoon salt

1 teaspoon cloves

1 teaspoon allspice

1 cup slivered almonds

SUBMITTED BY:
Eva Deitrich, Burgettstown

America's
HOME COOKING

Strufoli (Honey Clusters)

DIRECTIONS

Sift together the flour and salt into a bowl.
Add eggs one at a time and then the vanilla.
Turn the dough onto a lightly floured surface
and knead. Divide the dough in half. Roll each
half 1/4 inch thick. Cut dough with a pastry cutter into 1/4" wide strips. Use the palm of your
hand to roll strips to pencil thickness. Cut
pieces 1/4" long. Fry only as many pieces of
dough as will float uncrowded in deep fryer, 3-5
minutes or until lightly browned and puffed.
Drain on paper towels. Cook honey and sugar
in saucepan on low heat for 5 minutes.
Remove from heat and add fried dough pieces.
Stir until all pieces are coated and remove with
slotted spoon onto serving platter and set in
refrigerator until cool. Sprinkle with colored
decorating candies before serving.

INGREDIENTS

2 cups sifted flour
1/4 teaspoon salt
3 eggs
1/2 teaspoon vanilla
1 cup honey
1 tablespoon sugar
colored decorating candies

SUBMITTED BY:
Mary Ann Fennimore, Coral Springs

Wedding Cookies

DIRECTIONS

Preheat oven to 350 degrees. Mix all ingredients. Form tiny balls. Place on greased cookie sheet and bake at 350 degrees for 12 - 15 minutes.

INGREDIENTS

2 1/2 cups flour

1 cup sugar

1 egg yolk

1 cup shortening

8 oz package cream cheese

1 teaspoon vanilla

SUBMITTED BY:

Cornelia J. Salak, New Castle

Wine Cookies

DIRECTIONS

Preheat oven to 350 degrees. Mix together the oil, sugar and wine. Then at the baking powder and flour. Dough should not be too sticky (add flour if sticky, wine if stiff). Take a piece of dough, roll it into a log and pinch it into a circle about as round as a penny sized donut. Dip top of cookie in sugar. Bake at 350 for 15-20 minutes until tops are pinkish and bottoms are brown.

INGREDIENTS

1 cup oil

1 cup sugar

1 cup wine, any kind

1 teaspoon baking powder

4 cups flour

sugar for dipping

SUBMITTED BY:
Antoinette Jucha, in memory of Mrs. Zuchinski

Filled Cookies

Apricot Tarts

Directions

Shell: Preheat oven to 350 degrees. Grease several tassie pans well. Mix together the cornstarch, margarine, powdered sugar and flour until well blended. Place pinches of dough in tassie pans, making small cups from the outline of the pan. Fill each cup with 1 teaspoon of the apricot filling in each tart (See Notes). Add topping, bake for at least 15 minutes, until shell is nicely brown.

Topping: Mix the sugar, egg and coconut; place a bit of mixture on top of the filling in each shell.

Ingredients

Shell and filling:
1 tablespoon cornstarch
1 cup (2 sticks) margarine
1/2 cup powdered sugar
2 cups flour
12 oz jar apricot filling

Topping:
1/2 cup sugar
1 egg
1 1/2 cups shredded coconut

Notes

You can vary the tarts' flavors by filling the cups with different kinds of fruit preserves.

Submitted by:
Pat Steele, Greensburg

Caramel Tassies

DIRECTIONS

Combine all cookie ingredients. Refrigerate 3 hours or overnight. Preheat oven to 350 degrees. Divide dough into equal parts (approximately walnut sized) and put in tiny muffin cups; form the dough up around the sides of the cup. Bake at 350 degrees for 15 minutes. Let cool in cup trays. Makes 48 cookies.

Filling: Melt ingredients over low heat in double broiler; stirring constantly. Fill cooled cups. There is usually some filling leftover.

Frosting: Beat ingredients until creamy. After caramel has set, put frosting on top of cookies covering the caramel. Sprinkle chopped walnuts over cookies.

INGREDIENTS

6 oz cream cheese
1 cup butter or margarine
2 cups all purpose flour

Filling:
14 oz light caramels
1/2 cup evaporated milk

Frosting:
1/2 cup granulated sugar
1/2 cup shortening
1 teaspoon vanilla
1/2 cup evaporated milk
chopped walnuts

SUBMITTED BY:
Cathy Eppley, Boswe ll, PA

Cashew Drops

DIRECTIONS

Preheat oven to 400 degrees. Cream together butter and powdered sugar until light and fluffy. Stir in flour and salt until well combined. Add vanilla and half-and-half. Mix until all ingredients are thoroughly moistened. For each cookie, mold a teaspoonful of dough around a cashew nut; place on baking sheet. Bake for 10 to 12 minutes or until cookies are set, the top will be a pale golden color and the bottom will be light brown. Remove from oven and place cookies on wire rack to cool. Yields 30 cookies

INGREDIENTS

1/2 cup (1 stick) butter, softened

1/2 cup powdered sugar

1 3/4 cups flour

1/8 teaspoon salt

1/2 teaspoon vanilla extract

3 tablespoons half-and-half

whole cashews

America's HOME COOKING

Coconut Butterballs

DIRECTIONS

Preheat oven to 350 degrees. Cream margarine, sugar and vanilla until fluffy. Add flour and salt. If dough is too soft, chill until firm. Shape with fingers around a cherry, walnut or chocolate kiss to make a small ball. Beat egg white and water with a fork. Roll cookie in egg mixture, then roll in coconut. Bake at 350 degrees 15-18 minutes. Makes about 45 cookies.

INGREDIENTS

1 cup margarine or butter

1/2 cup sugar

2 teaspoons vanilla

2 cups flour

1/4 teaspoon salt

About 45 cherries, walnuts or chocolate kisses

1 egg white

1 tablespoon water

Coconut

SUBMITTED BY:
Eve Roha, Greensburg

Cookie Pops

DIRECTIONS

Preheat oven to 350 degrees. Mix sugars, margarine, peanut butter, vanilla, and egg. Add flour, baking soda, and salt. Mix well.

Insert sticks into candy bars and wrap dough completely around them. Bake on an ungreased cookie sheet for 13-16 minutes.

INGREDIENTS

1/2 cup brown sugar
1/2 cup sugar
1/2 cup soft margarine
1/2 cut peanut butter
1 teaspoon vanilla
1 egg
1 1/2 cups all purpose flour
1/2 teaspoon baking soda
1/4 teaspoon salt
20 fun size Milky Way or
Snickers bars
20 wooden popsicle sticks

SUBMITTED BY:
Nancy Polinsky, WQED Pittsburgh

93

Gateau Bon Bons

DIRECTIONS

Cream together margarine, cream cheese and sugar. Add egg, lemon juice and lemon rind. Beat with a mixer until light and fluffy. In a separate bowl, blend flour, baking powder, salt and baking soda together; add to creamed mixture. Mix thoroughly. Divide into four balls and chill. Preheat oven to 350 degrees; grease baking sheets. Take one ball from the refrigerator and roll it out 1/8 inch thick on a floured board. Cut 1 1/2-inch rounds. Arrange rounds on the cookie sheet, and put 1/2 teaspoon orange marmalade on each round. Place another round on top, sealing the edges of each pocket with floured fingers. Bake for 8 to 10 minutes.

Glaze: While the cookies are baking, mix together the powdered sugar and orange juice; glaze the baked cookies with this mixture.

INGREDIENTS

2/3 cup margarine or butter, softened

3 oz package cream cheese, softened

1 cup sugar

1 egg

1/2 teaspoon lemon juice

1 teaspoon finely grated lemon rind

2 cups flour

1/2 teaspoon baking powder

1/2 teaspoon salt

1/8 teaspoon baking soda

12 oz jar orange marmalade

Glaze:

1/2 cup powdered sugar

2 teaspoons orange juice

SUBMITTED BY:
Paula Sykes, Greensburg

America's HOME COOKING

Hidden Mint Cookies

DIRECTIONS

Preheat oven to 400 degrees. Mix sugars, margarine, shortening, vanilla and egg. Stir in flour, baking soda and salt. Shape one level tablespoonful of dough around each mint and place on a cookie sheet about 2 inches apart. Bake for 9 to 10 minutes or until golden brown. Immediately remove from cookie sheet; cool.

Glaze: Combine powdered sugar, milk and vanilla until smooth; tint with small amount of food coloring. Slather glaze over cookies.

Variation: One can substitute the mint wafers with mini peppermint patties for an even better treat. If you do this, use more batter per cookie to cover the larger mint.

NOTES

Omit baking soda and salt if using self-rising flour.

INGREDIENTS

1/2 cup granulated sugar

1/4 cup packed brown sugar

1/4 cup (1/2 stick) margarine or butter, softened

1/4 cup shortening

1/2 teaspoon vanilla extract

1 egg

1 2/3 cups all-purpose flour

1/2 teaspoon baking soda (See Note)

1/4 teaspoon salt

about 48 round or square pastel or chocolate wafer mints

Pastel Glaze:

1 1/2 cups powdered sugar

2 tablespoons milk

1 1/2 teaspoons vanilla extract

food coloring

SUBMITTED BY:
Shannon Reilly, Pittsburgh

Lemon Bites

DIRECTIONS

Filling: Combine first 6 ingredients in a saucepan. Cook over low heat, stirring constantly until thick. Remove from heat; add coconut and cool. Set aside for use as filling.

Sift together flour, cinnamon, baking soda and salt. Cream butter and sugar. Blend in egg and molasses. Add dry ingredients gradually and mix thoroughly. If desired, chill for easier handling.

Preheat oven to 350 degrees. Divide dough into four parts. Shape each into a 15 inch roll on a lightly sugared surface; flatten to a 15x2 1/2 inch strip. Spread 1/4 of filling down center of each strip. Fold in half and seal edges. Cut into 1 1/2 inch bars. Place on ungreased cookie sheet. Bake at 350 degrees for 12-15 minutes. Makes 3-4 dozen cookies.

INGREDIENTS

Filling:

2 slightly beaten eggs

1/2 cup sugar

1 tablespoon grated lemon rind

1/4 cup lemon juice

1 tablespoon butter

1/8 teaspoon salt

1 cup grated or chopped coconut

Dough:

2 1/4 cups sifted all purpose flour

1 teaspoon cinnamon

1/2 teaspoon baking soda

1/4 teaspoon salt

1/2 cup butter

1 cup sugar

1 unbeaten egg

1/4 cup molasses

SUBMITTED BY:
Annabelle Thomas, Pittsburgh

96

Peanut Blossoms

DIRECTIONS

Preheat oven to 375 degrees. Combine all ingredients (except sugar for rolling and chocolate kisses) in a large mixer bowl. Mix on lowest speed of mixer until dough forms. Shape dough into balls, using a rounded teaspoonful for each. Roll balls in sugar, and place the on cookie sheets. Bake for 10 to 12 minutes. Top each cookie immediately with a candy kiss, pressing down firmly with it so the cookie cracks around edge. Makes about 48 cookies.

INGREDIENTS

1 3/4 cups flour

1 teaspoon baking soda

1/2 teaspoon salt

1/2 cup sugar

1/2 cup firmly packed brown sugar

1/2 cup shortening

1/2 cup peanut butter

1 egg

2 tablespoons milk

1 teaspoon vanilla extract

Garnish:

sugar for rolling

milk chocolate candy kisses

SUBMITTED BY:
Mrs. C. Lapinski, Baden

97

Pecan Tassies

DIRECTIONS

Preheat oven to 350 degrees. Mix together ingredients for filling and let stand. Combine ingredients for dough. Roll into balls and press into tassie pans. Fill with nut mixture. Bake at 350 degrees for 20-25 minutes.

INGREDIENTS

Nut Filling:

2 1/2 cups brown sugar

4 large eggs

3 tablespoons butter

2 1/4 teaspoons vanilla

2 1/4 cups chopped pecans

Dough:

1 pound cream cheese

3 sticks oleo

3 cups flour

SUBMITTED BY:

Maria Cummings, Bridgeville

Strawberry Cream Cookies

DIRECTIONS

Have all ingredients at room temperature; preheat oven to 350 degrees. Cream butter, sugar and cream cheese; add vanilla and egg yolk. Mix well, then blend in the flour. Chill dough at least an hour. Shape into 1-inch balls. Using a floured thimble, press a hole in the center of each cookie and fill the 1/2 teaspoon of jam. Bake on cookie sheet for 10 to 12 minutes.

INGREDIENTS

1 cup (2 sticks) butter

1 cup sugar

3 oz package cream cheese

1 tablespoon vanilla extract

1 egg yolk

2 1/2 cups flour

strawberry jam

SUBMITTED BY:

Mrs. Helen Lamison, Carnegie

Surprise Holiday Hideaways

Directions

Preheat oven to 350 degrees. Cream short-ening, sugar, egg, milk and vanilla with electric mixer until well blended. Combine flour, bak-ing powder, salt and baking soda; beat into creamed mixture at low speed. Press dough into thin layer around cherries. Place 2 inches apart on ungreased baking sheet. Bake for 10 minutes and cool completely. Melt chocolate chips in microwave. Coat the cookie with the melted chocolate. Place cookies on waxed paper. Chill in refrigerator to set chocolate.

Ingredients

2/3 cup butter-flavored shortening

3/4 cup sugar

1 egg

1 tablespoon milk

1 teaspoon vanilla

1 3/4 cups flour

1 teaspoon baking powder

1/2 teaspoon salt

1/2 teaspoon baking soda

48 maraschino cherries, well drained and dried

1 bag chocolate chips

Submitted by:
Diane Miller, Richmond

America's
HOME COOKING

Vienna Tarts

DIRECTIONS

Chop dried apricots and add to the apricot preserves. Cook in a saucepan until preserves are thickened. Mix butter and cream cheese. Add flour and form into two balls. Refrigerate 4 hours or overnight.

Preheat oven to 350 degrees. Divide each ball into 4 smaller balls. Roll each ball out onto a floured surface to about 10" diameter circle. Cut the circle into 4 quarters. Place thickened apricot preserves in one quarter section and roll up toward center, tucking in sides slightly as you go. Do the same with the other quarters and repeat with the three other balls. Place the rolled tarts on a greased cookie sheet. Brush with beaten egg and sprinkle with chopped walnuts or sugar and cinnamon. Bake about 15 minutes until golden brown. Makes 32 tarts.

INGREDIENTS

2 sticks butter or margarine, softened

2 (3oz.) packages of cream cheese, softened

2 cups flour

12 oz. apricot preserves

1/2 cup dried apricots

1 egg, beaten

walnuts, chopped

sugar and cinnamon

SUBMITTED BY:

Chris Fennimore, WQED Pittsburgh

Cut-Out/Sugar Cookies

Cut Out Cookies

DIRECTIONS

Cream shortening well. Add sugar and egg; blend together. Sift baking powder, flour and salt together; slowly add to creamed mixture alternating with milk. Stir in vanilla. Chill well overnight.

Preheat oven to 350 degrees. Roll out cookie dough, being careful not to make it too thin. Cut out shapes using your favorite cookie cutters. Decorate. Bake at 350 degrees for 10-12 minutes.

INGREDIENTS

1/2 cup shortening

1 cup sugar

1 egg

2 tablespoons baking powder

2 1/2 cups flour

1/2 teaspoon salt

1/2 cup milk

1 teaspoon vanilla

NOTES

Try decorating the unbaked cookies by adding food coloring to egg yolks and using them as paint.

SUBMITTED BY:
Beckie Wagner, Masontown

Easy Sugar Cookies

DIRECTIONS

Dough: Preheat oven to 400 degrees. Combine all ingredients in large mixer bowl. Mix at low speed until a dough forms - 1 to 2 minutes. Roll out on a floured surface, one third at a time, to 1/8 inch thickness. Cut into desired shapes with floured cookie cutters or pastry wheel. Place on ungreased cookie sheet. Bake at 400 degrees for 5 to 8 minutes until golden brown. Frost and decorate as desired. Makes 72 - 84 cookies.

Frosting: Combine all ingredients for Creamy Batter Frosting in a large mixer bowl and beat until of spreading consistency.

INGREDIENTS

Dough:

3 cups flour

1 cup sugar

1 1/2 teaspoons baking powder

1/2 teaspoon salt

1 cup soft butter

1 egg

3 tablespoons milk

1 teaspoon vanilla extract

Creamy Batter Frosting:

1/4 cup soft butter

1 teaspoon vanilla extract

1/4 teaspoon salt

1 pound sifted powdered sugar

1/3 cup milk

SUBMITTED BY:
Cavita Barnes, Brownsville

America's
HOME COOKING

Favorite Christmas Cut-out Cookies

DIRECTIONS

Cream butter and sugar thoroughly. Add vanilla and orange rind. Add eggs, flour, baking soda and salt; mix well. Stir in nuts. Chill dough overnight.

Preheat oven to 375 degrees. Roll out very thin on floured pastry cloth and cut with favorite Christmas cutters. Bake on greased cookie sheet at 375 degrees for 8-10 minutes. Cool; ice and decorate as desired.

INGREDIENTS

1 cup butter

1 cup sugar

1 teaspoon vanilla

2 teaspoons grated orange rind

2 eggs

3 cups sifted flour

1/2 teaspoon baking soda

1 teaspoon salt

1 cup nuts

Icing and cookie decorations, if desired

SUBMITTED BY:
Viewer from Pittsburgh

Grandma Hattie's Sugar Cookies

DIRECTIONS

Preheat oven to 375 degrees. Mix together the sugars, shortening and butter; add eggs and mix well. Add flour, baking powder and nutmeg. Dissolve the soda in the buttermilk and add to mixture. Add the vanilla and nuts; mix. Mixing with the hands, add enough flour to bring the dough to the consistency of pie dough. Roll out dough and cut in desired shapes; but don't roll too thin. Bake about 7 minutes or until the cookies are brown on bottom.

INGREDIENTS

1 cup sugar

1 cup brown sugar

1/2 cup shortening

1/2 cup (1 stick) butter or margarine

2 eggs

3 cups flour, plus more to reach consistency

2 teaspoons baking powder

1 teaspoon nutmeg

1 teaspoon baking soda

1 cup buttermilk

1 teaspoon vanilla extract

1 cup chopped walnuts

NOTES

Variations: Sprinkle sugar on each cookie before baking; put a raisin in center of each; or frost the cookies as desired.

SUBMITTED BY:
Olive Rhoads, Alliance, Ohio

America's
HOME COOKING

Grandma's Sugar Cookies

DIRECTIONS

Preheat oven to 350 degrees. In a large bowl, beat shortening, sugar and brown sugar until light and fluffy. Add vanilla and egg; beat well. Lightly spoon flour into measuring cup; level off. Stir in flour, baking soda and salt; mix well. Shape dough into 3/4 inch balls. Using the bottom of a glass that has been dipped in sugar, press cookies to 1/8 inch thickness. Bake at 350 degrees for 7-12 minutes or until light golden brown. Cool one minute and remove from cookie sheet. Makes 5 dozen cookies.

INGREDIENTS

1 cup shortening

1/2 cup sugar

1/2 cup firmly packed brown sugar

1/2 teaspoon vanilla

1 egg

2 cups all-purpose or unbleached flour

1/2 teaspoon baking soda

1/2 teaspoon salt

1/4 cup sugar

NOTES

For the holidays, dip bottom of the glass in colored sugar.

SUBMITTED BY:

Debbie Ayres, Bridgeville

Novelty Cookies

Candy Cane Cookies

DIRECTIONS

Preheat oven to 350 degrees. Combine shortening, margarine, powdered sugar, egg, almond extract and vanilla. Sift together the flour and salt; add to original mixture until well blended. After dividing the dough in half, add food coloring to one half. Take small bits of each color of dough separately and roll into a long roll. Pinch tops together and twist into a striped candy cane. Cut 4-inch strips of dough, bending each at top to resemble a cane. Place on cookie sheet and bake at 350 degrees for 15 minutes.

INGREDIENTS

1 cup shortening

1/2 cup margarine

1 cup powdered sugar

1 egg

1 1/2 teaspoons almond extract

1 teaspoon vanilla extract

2 1/2 cups flour

1 teaspoon salt

red food coloring

SUBMITTED BY:

Edith Stimpson, Hickory

Chop Suey Cookies

DIRECTIONS

Heat water in the bottom of a double boiler. Melt the chocolate morsels and peanut butter in the double boiler; mix. Add noodles and stir until they are well covered. Drop by teaspoonful onto waxed paper, and cool in refrigerator.

INGREDIENTS

12 oz package butterscotch or chocolate morsels

1 1/2 cups peanut butter

2 (5 oz) cans chow mein noodles

SUBMITTED BY:
Margaret Meister, Pittsburgh

America's
HOME COOKING

Coconut Macaroons

DIRECTIONS

Preheat oven to 350 degrees. Grease two large cookie sheets. In a medium bowl mix the coconut, milk, vanilla and almond extracts and a pinch of salt with a spoon until well blended. Arrange the cherry halves on cookies sheets, each several inches apart. Drop the dough by rounded teaspoonfuls onto each cherry half. Bake to 12 to 15 minutes, until golden at edges. Remove immediately from cookie sheets and cool on wire racks. Makes about 3 1/2 dozen.

INGREDIENTS

3 1/2 cups (10 oz) flaked coconut

14-oz can sweetened condensed milk

1 teaspoon vanilla extract

1/2 teaspoon almond extract

pinch of salt

23 glazed cherries, halved

NOTES

To freeze these cookies, wrap them well. They keep for up to 3 months.

SUBMITTED BY:
Ellie Diulus, Penn Hills

Hamburger Cookies

DIRECTIONS

For each hamburger cookie, spread 1/2 teaspoon of frosting on flat side of 1 vanilla wafer. Place 1 teaspoon coconut and 1 mint cookie on frosting. Spread flat side of second vanilla wafer with 1/2 teaspoon frosting; place frosting side down on mint cookie. Brush top of hamburger with honey; sprinkle with sesame seed. Repeat to make 5 more cookies. Makes 6 cookies.

INGREDIENTS

2 tablespoons vanilla frosting

12 vanilla wafers

2 tablespoons green coconut (see note)

1 cup chocolate-covered round mint cookies or patties

honey, warmed

sesame seeds

NOTES

To tint coconut, place coconut and 1 to 2 drops of green food coloring in jar or heavy resealable plastic bag. Seal and shake until coconut is uniformly colored.

SUBMITTED BY:
Debbie Ayres, Bridgeville

Ice Cream Cookies

DIRECTIONS

Melt butter in a medium sauce pan; remove from heat. Add ice cream, stir until melted. Add the flour and salt. Stir briskly until the mixture forms a ball and pulls away from the side of the pan. Refrigerate for about 15 minutes, stir again. Divide the dough in half. Wrap in waxed paper and flatten each piece into a square; refrigerate for 3 or more hours.

Melt the butter, mix sugar and cinnamon together for the filling. Lightly flour rolling pin and rolling surface. Taking half the dough out of the refrigerator, roll it into a 12 inch square. It should be paper thin. Brush with 1/2 the melted butter. Stop 1/2 inch from the edge. Sprinkle with 1/2 the sugar mixture and 1/2 the raisins and 1/2 the nuts. With your fingers, pat a little bit of water on one edge of the square. Starting at the opposite end, roll the dough very tightly to the wet end. Wrap the dough in waxed paper and place on a cookie sheet or cutting board. Repeat the procedure with remaining dough. Chill overnight.

Preheat oven to 350 degrees. Unwrap roll and cut into 1/2 inch slices. Bake for 25 minutes or until lightly colored. Cookie should be crisp all the way through when cooled.

INGREDIENTS

1/2 cup (1 stick) butter
1/2 cup vanilla ice cream
1 cup flour
1/8 teaspoon salt

Filling:
2 tablespoons butter
1/4 cup sugar
2 teaspoons cinnamon
1/2 cup raisins, chopped
1 cup walnuts, chopped

SUBMITTED BY:
Emma Washington, Pittsburgh

Mom's Pinwheel Cookies

DIRECTIONS

Cream sugar, salt and butter or margarine thoroughly. Beat egg and vanilla extract into creamed ingredients until light and fluffy. Sift together flour and baking powder. Gradually stir into creamed mixture. Divide dough in half. Roll half of dough on lightly floured waxed paper to form 9x12 inch rectangle 1/8 inch thick; set aside. Blend cocoa into unrolled dough; roll second rectangle from chocolate dough. Turn chocolate layer onto vanilla layer; remove waxed paper. Trim rough edge. Roll two layers of dough a like jelly roll. Wrap in waxed paper and chill several hours until firm.

Preheat oven to 350 degrees. Slice 1/8 inch cookies from rolls with sharp knife. Place on lightly greased cookie sheet. Bake for 8-10 minutes or until brown. Remove to cookie rack. Yield about 6 dozen cookies.

INGREDIENTS

1 cup packed light brown sugar

1/4 teaspoon salt

1/2 cup (1 stick) butter or margarine

1 egg

1 teaspoon vanilla extract

2 cups all-purpose flour

1 teaspoon baking powder

2 tablespoons cocoa

SUBMITTED BY:
Marilyn Rollin and Amy Rollin, Pittsburgh

America's
HOME COOKING

Pecan Tarts

DIRECTIONS

Preheat oven to 350 degrees. Cut together butter, cream cheese and flour using a pastry cutter. Line a small muffin pan with dough; set aside. Cream together eggs, brown sugar, melted butter and vanilla; fold in nuts. Spoon filling evenly into muffin pan, filling each cup 1/2 to 3/4 full. If desired, place 1/2 pecan on top of each tart before baking. Bake at 350 degrees about 30 minutes until tarts are lightly brown.

INGREDIENTS

1/2 pound (2 sticks) butter

8 oz package cream cheese

2 1/2 cups flour

3 eggs

2 1/2 cups light brown sugar

4 tablespoons melted butter

1 teaspoon vanilla

2 1/2 cups pecans, finely chopped

Halved pecans for garnish, if desired

SUBMITTED BY:
Dorothy J. Shaner, Stoneboro

Peggy's Piano Keys

DIRECTIONS

Preheat oven to 375 degrees. Sift together flour and baking powder and set aside. Cream butter, sugar and salt. Add egg and vanilla to butter mixture and blend in. Add sifted ingredients to the butter mixture gradually until well blended. Using cookie press or pastry bag, pipe onto ungreased cookie sheets, using plain tip to achieve smooth top. Bake 10 minutes cool completely.

For Black Keys: melt chocolate and butter together. Dip one of end of cooled cookie into warm mixture. Drain and cool on piece of waxed paper. Allow chocolate to harden.

For White Part of Key: cover chocolate end with waxed paper then using sifter or small stainer, gently tap confectioners sugar onto exposed part of the cookie. OR: drizzle or dip non-chocolate end into glaze of sugar, lemon juice and lemon rind; add enough milk or water to thin mixture. Allow to harden on waxed paper.

INGREDIENTS

2 1/2 cups sifted flour
1/2 teaspoon baking powder
1 cup butter
3/4 cup sugar
dash of salt
1 egg
1 tablespoon vanilla

Icing:
2 squares Baker's chocolate
2 tablespoons butter

Glaze:
1 cup powdered sugar
juice of 1 lemon
grated rind of 1 lemon
milk

SUBMITTED BY:
Peggy Stewart, Coraopolis

116

Rum Balls

DIRECTIONS

Combine crumbs, nuts or coconut, sugar, cocoa, syrup and rum. Let stand 30 minutes. Shape into balls. Roll in instant coffee, colored sugar or nuts. Store in airtight container for several weeks to improve flavor. Makes about 3 dozen 1 inch balls.

INGREDIENTS

2 cups vanilla wafer crumbs

1 cup finely chopped nuts or coconut

1 cup confectioners sugar

2 tablespoons dry unsweetened cocoa

2 tablespoons light corn syrup

1/2 cup rum, brandy or bourbon

instant coffee, colored sugar and/or finely chopped nuts

NOTES

This recipe is not for children or anyone who should not consume alcohol. The spirits are not cooked and the cookies can be potent.

SUBMITTED BY:
Eve Roha, Greensburg

Index

Index

Index

Index

Index